Reviews of
How Love Poems Work: from William Shakespeare to Bob Dylan

Connie Post
Poet Laureate for Livermore, California 2005 to 2009.
5 out of 5 stars. A wonderful exploration of Love Poetry.
In this book, Sandra Roe examines love poetry. She does so in an eloquent way, providing the history of each poet she explores. This books reminds us why we often seek love poems, what they do for us and why. I liked learning more about the history of each poet and learning the "how and why" of each of their poems. The author provides important context for each work examined in the book. It is also an easy read and one can pick up any chapter they are interested in at any time. I enjoyed her final section of Bob Dylan, reminding us the love poems come in many shapes and sizes. This book pleasantly reminds us why we fall in love with love poetry, after all. By Connie Post, Author of Floodwater (Glass Lyre Press 2014)

Robin
4 out of 5 stars. Great read.
This is a beautifully produced compact book full of love. It's written with love and is about love poetry through the ages. The author gives some analysis of Shakespeare's sonnets, Donne's love poetry, Marlowe, WH Auden, Robert Burns and Elizabeth Barrett Browning all the way to Bob Dylan's lyrical songs - so there is a feast through the ages to nourish the reader. The author's analysis is insightful and the writing is clear and precise. Highly recommended!

How Love Poems Work:

from William Shakespeare to Bob Dylan

Sandra Roe

First published in 2018 by
Sandra Roe
PO Box 219
Como WA 6152
Australia

This book is copyright. Apart from any fair dealing for the purpose of private research, criticism or review, as permitted under the Copyright Act, no part may be reproduced by any process without written permission. Enquiries should be made to the publisher. The moral rights of the author have been asserted.

Copyright © Sandra Roe

Book cover design by Estella Vukovic of 99designs.
Proofreading by Victor Nicoli and Sue Emmett.
Formatting by Polgarus Studio.

For Victor

Contents

Introduction: A Short History of Love Poetry 1

William Shakespeare 7
Christopher Marlowe 17
John Donne, Andrew Marvell and the
Metaphysical Poets 21
Robert Burns 37
Elizabeth Barrett Browning 41
Robert Browning 45
Christina Rossetti 51
W.H. Auden 63
Bob Dylan 69

Glossary of Key Literary Terms 73
References 81
Acknowledgements 83
Also by Sandra Roe 85
If you enjoyed this book 87
About the author 89

INTRODUCTION
A SHORT HISTORY OF LOVE POETRY

What is it about love poetry that we love so much? Why is poetry such a popular medium for expressing love? This short book will consider these questions by taking a look at some of the finest love poetry of the English language.

Love is one of the earliest and most enduring subjects of poetry. Indeed, love poetry may be as old as poetry itself. The oldest surviving poems – some of them up to four thousand years old, dating from the ancient Sumerian period – are poems of divine and romantic love.

The complex, concentrated language of a poem, with its interacting layers of image, idea and music, has a lot in common with the complexity and intensity of love. The poem is an apt medium for expressing love because, like love, poems can be beautiful *and* sad, wonderful *and* difficult. A poem itself is, we might say, a metaphor for love. In both, more is being said than is said.

The popularity of love poetry throughout the ages suggests that readers crave literary encounters with love. We want to have our feeling and experiences reflected back at us in words. Reading poems, we anticipate a glimmer of recognition. We are consoled because we feel understood. In that moment of sympathy we are inspired, even changed. This empathic, healing connection is encapsulated by the Ancient Greek word *catharsis*, a word we still use today when talking about the power of art to heal old wounds.

In the next few paragraphs we'll take a whistle-stop tour of love poetry's modern historical development, beginning in thirteenth-century Italy. We'll then spend some time with individual poets, beginning with Shakespeare in sixteenth-century England. We'll then look at some poems by the finest writers in the English language. Their verse will demonstrate the different ways in which poets have written about love.

But love poetry is never only about love. Its meanings reach into other areas of our lives. We'll see this especially in the later poets, like W.H. Auden and Bob Dylan.

* * *

Today, we tend to think of writing poetry as a personal, private act, but this has not always been the case. In thirteenth-century Europe, when society was dominated by feudalism and the Roman Catholic church, the troubadours presented their tales of love for the court of the aristocracy, singing in the vernacular (that is, in the everyday language of the people, rather than in Latin). These were stylised, predictable, repetitive poems. They were written to be read aloud, not in silence on the page. They were almost always addressed to a lady of high birth, who was portrayed as beautiful, moral, and unattainable. There was a necessary distance between poet and subject: the lady's high social status and the poet's lower standing created an unbridgeable gulf, which the poet filled with desire.

In her detailed account of the development of the earliest love poetry in Europe, *The Idiom of Love: Love Poetry from the Earliest Sonnets to the 17th Century*, Judy Sproxton explains that "the state of mind attributed by the poet/persona to himself is consistent with the state of subservience promoted in the period by both Church and feudal system [...] The Church and feudal society were all powerful." The average troubador poet "describes himself as essentially centreless, motivated only by the adoration of the lady". In short, they lacked the degree of self-consciousness more common to later love poems, like Shakespeare's (as we shall see very shortly).

Alongside the lyrics of the troubadours, another type of lyric poetry was emerging in thirteenth-century Europe. In the court of Frederik II of Sicily, a style of poetry was flourishing that, with its emphasis on the personal response to individual experience, anticipated Europe's budding Renaissance: the sonnet. The invention of the sonnet is credited to the lawyer and love-poet Giacomo da Lentino.

Lentino took the octave (an eight-line poem used in traditional Sicilian peasant songs) and added a sestet (of six lines). This new fourteen-line poem brought with it a new way of writing and thinking, a more self-conscious, reflexive, and personal poetry. In the sonnet, "the struggle is within the heart of the lover himself," writes Sproxton, who provides a good description of how a sonnet works:

> The sonnet combines, in the short space of fourteen lines, both past and present. The present experience of the writer is presented in the first eight lines, as a difficulty in which he is currently involved. Through a sudden change of perspective in the concluding sestet, another dimension is added: that of the writer's reflection on his experience. The pattern of the sonnet promotes reflection. Its content is not simply presented: it is also resolved, in a very particular way, which only the writer himself could achieve. The momentum of the sonnet came from the writer's insistence on some kind of resolution. Unlike the troubadours' song, it was not compiled to suit the taste of an audience, formed by habit. It spoke of emotion confronted and, in some highly personal way, resolved. Through the creation of a sonnet through his own depiction of emotional conflict, the writer was able at the same time to draw on the personal response of his reader. It was an essentially introspective, intimate way of writing.

Francesco Petrarch (1304–1374) was an Italian poet, scholar, and man of letters. He is regarded by many as the earliest major practitioner of the sonnet. He refined and popularised the form, which has come to be known as the Petrarchan sonnet. In so doing he was influenced by ancient writers, especially the Roman politician Cicero (106–43 BC) and the Algerian theologian St Augustine (AD 354–430), learning from them a respect for the value of individual experience.

Petrarch was interested in recreating the intensity of love in his writing. He focused on both the experience itself and on the compelling consciousness it provoked. He is famous for his striking use of images, which became seminal in their capacity to evoke the experience of love. For instance, in Poem 2, love is seen as a "blow" which strikes when the lover is unprepared. With his bow, Cupid shoots an arrow through the lover's eyes and into the heart.

Two hundred years later, the sonnet finally makes its way into the English language, introduced in the early sixteenth century by English poet-politician Thomas Wyatt (1503–1542). It quickly became the form of choice for poets in Elizabethan England. William Shakespeare (1564–1616) developed the form further by widening the scope of its images. The imagery in his sonnets displays unprecedented complexity and richness. Much as Petrarch's influence on the Italian sonnet created a permanent association between the form and his name, the English version of the form has come to be known as the Shakespearean sonnet.

Let's look at some of Shakespeare's famous sonnets and see how they work. Afterwards, we'll read some poems by Shakespeare's contemporaries, Christopher Marlowe (1564–1593) and John Donne (1572–1631). We'll then work our way to the present day, via Andrew Marvell (1621–1678), Robert Burns (1759–1796), Elizabeth Barrett Browning (1806–1861), Robert Browning (1812–1889), Christina Rossetti (1830–1894), and W.H. Auden (1907–1973), ending with the love lyrics of Bob Dylan (1941–).

WILLIAM SHAKESPEARE

<u>Sonnet 18</u>

Shall I compare thee to a summer's day?
Thou art more lovely and more temperate.
Rough winds do shake the darling buds of May,
And summer's lease hath all too short a date.
Sometime too hot the eye of heaven shines,
And often is his gold complexion dimmed;
And every fair from fair sometime declines,
By chance, or nature's changing course, untrimmed;
But thy eternal summer shall not fade,
Nor lose possession of that fair thou ow'st,
Nor shall death brag thou wand'rest in his shade,
When in eternal lines to Time thou grow'st.
    So long as men can breathe, or eyes can see,
    So long lives this, and this gives life to thee.

In Elizabethan England, when Shakespeare was writing, the sonnet was the form of choice for lyric poets who wanted to engage with the theme of love. The sonnet's association with love was established by its early Italian practitioners, as described in the Introduction. Ever since, a poet has been able to create a romantic atmosphere simply by choosing the sonnet form, with its recognisable fourteen-line structure.

Unlike the Petrarchan sonnet, the Shakespearean sonnet is divided into four parts. The first three parts are quatrains (four-line stanzas), rhymed ABAB. The fourth part is a couplet, rhymed CC. The Shakespearean sonnet is often used to develop a sequence of metaphors or ideas, one in each quatrain. The third quatrain generally acts as a "volta", a shift in thought or perspective, a poetic turn. The final couplet is either a summary of, or a new take on, what has been said so far.

On first reading, Shakespeare's sonnets can seem intimidatingly difficult. It takes effort, attention and experience to reach an understanding of their many levels of meaning, their references and images, and their complex music and structure. They require careful reading, but the effort is more than rewarded.

Sonnet 18, also known as "Shall I Compare Thee to a Summer's Day?", comes from Shakespeare's so-called Fair Youth sequence. It is one of his best-loved sonnets, and perhaps the most famous lyric poem in the English language. Its popularity may be partly because of its simplicity, its directness, and its striking and original imagery. On the surface, it is simply a statement of praise about the beauty of the beloved. But close reading reveals its complexity and richness, as well as a fundamental paradox at the heart of the poem.

It begins with a question: "Shall I Compare to a Summer's Day?" Then the speaker lists the faults of a summer's day, implying the beloved's superior beauty. With its "rough winds" that shake the "darling buds of May", summer is over too soon, its "lease" cut all too short. The beloved is lovelier than this, more gentle, and more constant.

In the second quatrain, lines 5 to 8, the speaker points out the flaws of the sun, which on some days shines too brightly and on others is dimmed by clouds. Every beautiful ("fair") thing eventually fades from beauty, either by ill luck ("chance") or due to natural decay over the course of time ("nature's changing course untrimm'd"). In lines 5 to 8, Shakespeare subtly shifts from a concern with mutability in the first eight lines to a concern for eternity.

In lines 9 to 12 (the third quatrain), the speaker continues to compare the beloved, a young man, with summer. Unlike the sun, which waxes and wanes, the youth's "eternal summer shall not fade". He owns ("ow'st") his beauty, and therefore cannot lose it. But there is a hint too here of *owed*, beauty as something borrowed from nature that must be repaid (that is, when the beloved eventually passes away and returns to the earth). This awareness of the beloved's physical mortality is developed in the next two lines, when the speaker says that, rather than wandering in death's "shade", his beloved is growing towards immortality, thanks to the "eternal lines" of the poem.

The final couplet is a summary of the speaker's position and a conclusion of his argument. As long as the human race continues to exist, and reads poetry, Shakespeare's poem ("this") survives and "gives life" to the young man by keeping his memory alive.

But Sonnet 18 is not simply a comparison of summer and the beloved. In *The Art of Shakespeare's Sonnets*, Helen Vendler suggests that this sonnet is an example of "one of Shakespeare's greatest compositional powers":

> his capacity to confer greater and greater mental scope on any whim of the imagination, enacting that widening gradually, so that the experience of reading a poem becomes the experience of pushing back the horizons of thought.

Vendler charts this "inexorable widening of scope and deepening of gravity" over the course of the first twelve lines:

> thee and a day (1-2)
> a month (May) (3)
> end of a season (Summer) (4)
> the eye of heaven (sun, ordainer of seasons) (5)
> the weather itself (hot or dimmed) (6)

> the <u>decline</u> of <u>every</u> beauty (7)
> the operations of <u>chance</u> (8)
> the <u>changing course</u> of <u>nature</u> (8)
> an <u>eternal</u> summer (9)
> an un<u>fading</u> <u>fairness</u> (9–10)
> the foiling of <u>Death</u> (11)
> <u>eternal</u> art (12)

Vendler also highlights a fundamental paradox in Sonnet 18: "To be more temperate than natural loveliness, one must escape natural chance and the cycle of change." Shakespeare, she suggests, "entwines, in perpetual paradox, the brevity of love, temporal truth, and the fragile strength of art before its extinction."

Let's look at another classic Shakespeare sonnet, number 147.

<u>Sonnet 147</u>

> My love is as a fever, longing still
> For that which longer nurseth the disease,
> Feeding on that which doth preserve the ill,
> Th' uncertain sickly appetite to please.
> My reason, the physician to my love,
> Angry that his prescriptions are not kept,
> Hath left me, and I desperate now approve
> Desire is death, which physic did except.
> Past cure I am, now reason is past care,

And frantic-mad with evermore unrest;
My thoughts and my discourse as madmen's are,
At random from the truth vainly expressed:
> For I have sworn thee fair, and thought thee bright,
> Who art as black as hell, as dark as night.

Here we have another Shakespearean sonnet: it is made up of three quatrains followed by a rhyming couplet, it has the typical rhyme scheme of ABAB CDCD EFEF GG, and is composed in iambic pentameter. This one belongs to the so-called Dark Lady sequence (sonnets 127 to 154). Coming after the Fair Youth sonnets, the Dark Lady sonnets are associated with a woman with dark physical and moral features, neither classically beautiful nor of high social status. In this respect Shakespeare is writing against the fashion of the day. Most poems of that era address fair, virginal young women of high social standing.

Sonnet 147 reveals a conflict within its speaker, one familiar to many of us even today. There is a tension between the desire for the sin or ill which makes one sickly, and the knowledge that the thing desired (in this case, the speaker's beloved) is the very thing causing trouble. The Ancient Greeks called this feeling *akrasia*.

In the first quatrain the speaker has been "infected", so to speak, by his beloved. It seems to take the form of a desired parasite feeding on his sense and reason. The speaker links together the concepts of love and disease. His love and wantonness is weakening him to the point where his lust has taken on its own force, like a fever.

In the second quatrain, his reason (represented metaphorically by "physician") offers the speaker a way of easing his fever. But reason abandons him, as he is so foolish in body and mind. Without reason, the illness and fever are doomed to take him over completely, and death is the only possible outcome.

In the third quatrain the speaker continues to describe his sickness. But the tone shifts in the final couplet, and the speaker begins to address his beloved directly. Not fondly, as most sonnets would, but with bitterness. The speaker's harsh indictment comes as a surprise, but it gives credence to his "frantic-mad" state of mind. On the other hand, Helen Vendler has suggested that the clarity of the language "confers a kind of nobility on the "frantic-mad" speaker, who suddenly enters a moment of utter lucidity even while he is offering an instance of his own past madness." But for Vendler, it is the change of address itself that is crucial, because "the contrast between past-extending-into present and the present of "now" gives the poem its sense of temporal extension marking character disintegration."

Before we move on, let's look at one more sonnet by the greatest poet of the English language.

Sonnet 116

Let me not to the marriage of true minds
Admit impediments. Love is not love
Which alters when it alteration finds,
Or bends with the remover to remove:
O, no! it is an ever-fixed mark,
That looks on tempests and is never shaken;
It is the star to every wandering bark,
Whose worth's unknown, although his height be taken.
Love's not Time's fool, though rosy lips and cheeks
Within his bending sickle's compass come;
Love alters not with his brief hours and weeks,
But bears it out even to the edge of doom.
    If this be error and upon me proved,
    I never writ, nor no man ever loved.

Sonnet 116 is usually read as Shakespeare's attempt at defining true love. At first glance, it might appear to be fairly straightforward, with a relatively simple structure, each quatrain attempting to describe what love is or is not. But as usual it contains hidden depths and dimensions.

The speaker begins by stating that he would not "admit impediments" to "the marriage of true minds". In their rhythm and tone these lines echo the Christian marriage service. He says that love cannot be true if it changes for any reason. Love should be constant, through any difficulties. He makes a seafaring reference, stating that love is like the north star to sailors. He says that love should not fade with time, that it should be an "ever-fixed mark."

In the final couplet, the speaker seems to state that if he is proved wrong, then he will take back what he has written, and no man has truly loved. He seems to be stating that he is certain that he is right in what he is saying in his interpretation of true love.

However, some scholars have argued that the theme has been misunderstood. Helen Vendler, for example, has commented that the "prevalence of negatives suggests that this poem is not a definition, but rather a rebuttal – and all rebuttals encapsulate the argument they refute." She goes on to say that the sonnet's iambic rhythm belies the general reading, and the sonnet's meaning is emphasized by the stress falling on "me" in the first line: "Let _me_ not to the marriage…"

This sonnet's contemporary popularity was given a boost when it featured in director Ang Lee's film adaptation of Jane Austen's novel *Sense and Sensibility*. Willoughby asks Marianne what her favourite sonnet is. When she tells him that it is Sonnet 116, he recites a few lines. (You can view this scene by searching for "Shakespeare in Sense and Sensibility (Sonnet 116)" on YouTube.) Having fallen in love with Willoughby, Marianne is heart broken when he marries someone else who is extremely wealthy. (You can view the scene by searching for "Sense and Sensibility – Love is not Love" on YouTube.) Interestingly, the sonnet does not appear in Austen's novel. The screenwriter, Emma Thompson, added it.

CHRISTOPHER MARLOWE

Christopher Marlowe (1564–1593) was most famous for his plays, especially *Dr Faustus*. Perhaps his most famous poem is "A Passionate Shepherd to His Love", a clever and flexible example of a pastoral lyric.

A Passionate Shepherd to his Love

Come live with me and be my love,
And we will all the pleasures prove,
That Valleys, groves, hills, and fields,
Woods, or steepy mountain yields.

And we will sit upon the Rocks,
Seeing the Shepherds feed their flocks,
By shallow Rivers to whose falls
Melodious birds sing Madrigals.

And I will make thee beds of Roses
And a thousand fragrant posies,
A cap of flowers, and a kirtle
Embroidered all with leaves of Myrtle;

A gown made of the finest wool
Which from our pretty Lambs we pull;
Fair lined slippers for the cold,
With buckles of the purest gold;

A belt of straw and Ivy buds,
With Coral clasps and Amber studs:
And if these pleasures may thee move,
Come live with me, and be my love.

The Shepherds' Swains shall dance and sing
For thy delight each May-morning:
If these delights thy mind may move,
Then live with me, and be my love.

On first reading, this pastoral poem may seem light and insubstantial. Closer analysis, however, reveals that it is a clever and flexible poem. As a pastoral lyric, it creates an idealized vision of rural life. The pastoral is a mode of literature rather than a genre, and it places the complex life into a simple one. It does this by depicting rural life in the English countryside, among shepherds and other rustic workers, in an unrealistic and romanticised manner. In ancient times, pastoral poetry grew out of the folk songs and ceremonies that honoured the classical gods. The earliest surviving pastoral poetry was written by Theocritus in the third century BC. The setting in a pastoral poem is always a beautiful place in nature. They tend to be written from the point of view of shepherds or other rural workers, but are always penned by highly sophisticated urban poets.

"A Passionate Shepherd to his Love" is written in regular iambic tetrameter (di *dum* di *dum* di *dum* di *dum*) and the meter gives meaning and music to the poem. But the metre is not strict. For example, in line 6 ("seeing the Shepherds feed their flocks") the poet inverts the first iamb; in line 9 ("and I will make thee beds of Roses") he adds an extra beat to the end of the line; and in line 10 ("And a thousand fragrant posies") he shifts from iambic into trochaic metre (*di* dum *di* dum *di* dum *di* dum). Temporary shifts in metre make the poem lighter to read, musical and regular but not rigid or predictable.

In the first stanza, the speaker gently and directly calls his love to come with him and "pleasures prove." The poem then goes on to detail what these pleasures will be. The speaker implies that the entire countryside in England will prove to contain a vast array of pleasures. In the second stanza, the speaker suggests that the lovers will find entertainment while sitting on rocks or by rivers. They will be watching shepherds feeding their flocks, or listening to waterfalls and bird song. Such a vision of bounteous earth is a common theme in pastoral poetry.

In the third, fourth and fifth stanzas, there is a list of delights that the shepherd will make for his love. It now becomes clear that the speaker is not himself a shepherd at all. He seems instead to be a feudal landowner who employs shepherds. Some of the delights listed (such as "buckles of the purest gold" and "coral clasps") would not be easily obtained by a tenant shepherd. They could only be procured by a member of the gentry or a town merchant. This is another convention of pastoral poetry: it celebrates the rural life of manual labour, but the poet is assumed to be noble, or at least above manual labour. The fantasy of bucolic paradise is entirely idealised. Marlowe's shepherd is not a real person, merely a device to celebrate an old poetic ideal in verse.

JOHN DONNE, ANDREW MARVELL
AND THE METAPHYSICAL POETS

The metaphysical poets were a loose group of seventeenth-century writers whose work is characterised by the inventive use of conceits. With an emphasis on the spoken rather than lyrical quality of verse, on the solitary voice rather than on musical accompaniment, their style marked a shift from the smoothness of conventional Elizabethan love poetry. But love is a common theme in metaphysical poetry too. Poems of this period are intellectual, passionate, and emotionally engaging, and we enjoy their cleverness, humour, richness of paradox and vibrant language.

During the English Renaissance, which roughly spanned the sixteenth century, there was renewed interest in classical literature, history and moral philosophy from the ancient Greek and Roman periods. Geographical exploration was thriving, and there were significant political changes, including the gradual replacement of feudalism with legislative central government. It was a time of uncertainty as new ideas challenged old beliefs, especially the centuries-old understanding of the cosmos.

In the twenty-first century we tend to think of space as a three-dimensional void in which things move freely. But up until the seventeenth-century, most people thought space was material, forceful, meaningful, and arranged in concentric circles.

It was a widely held belief for many centuries that Earth was at the centre of the cosmos, and that the cosmos was arranged in concentric spheres. The sphere enclosed by the orbit of the moon was known as the sublunary sphere, where everything was living and dying, moving in rectilinear motion: going up and down, coming together and falling apart. Matter was composed of the four elements – earth, fire, air and water – each of which belonged to its own sublunary realm. Above the sublunary sphere was the celestial sphere, which was made from simpler, purer stuff. The heavenly bodies in this sphere lasted for eternity and moved in a regular pattern, and they were thought to be pure because they moved in a circular motion. Life and love were thought imperfect because they only existed in the lineal path of the moon.

In the seventeenth century these old ideas about the space and the cosmos were being challenged. Giordano Bruno (1548–

1600), a radical thinker of the Copernican school, argued that there were no fixed spheres, no limits, and no circumferences. This was a new idea – that space is undifferentiated, that place does not affect the nature of things and does not affect their being at rest or in motion. At the same time, the development of cartography provided a new way of seeing space in two rather than three dimensions.

This is all important historical context to bear in mind while reading the great poems of the period, including those of John Donne (1572–1631) and Andrew Marvell (1621–1678). These different ways of imagining space – the cosmographic and the new cartographic – play against each other in Donne's verse. The traditional interpretation of space informs the background of his spatial imagination. He imagined metaphysical relationships spatially, in terms of spheres, circles, centres and circumferences. Space took shape and meaning from the forms that filled it.

Donne is widely considered the most important of the metaphysical poets. He is a master of metaphysical conceit (an extended metaphor combining two disparate ideas within a single concept, often using imagery and paradox, and carrying multiple levels of meaning). Donne wrote with strong sensuality and vibrant language, balancing the solemnity of his themes with wit and humour. He wrote most of his poems early in his life, penning his love poems in his twenties. Though largely unpublished in his lifetime, he circulated his writing widely among friends in manuscript form.

His poems may seem difficult at first glance, but they are accessible and rewarding upon careful reading, and with some knowledge of the cultural context of seventeenth-century England, outlined above. So let's look at one of Donne's most famous poems, 'To His Mistress Going to Bed'.

<u>To His Mistress Going to Bed</u>

Come, Madam, come, all rest my powers defy,
Until I labour, I in labour lie.
The foe oft-times having the foe in sight,
Is tir'd with standing though he never fight.
Off with that girdle, like heaven's Zone glistering,
But a far fairer world encompassing.
Unpin that spangled breastplate which you wear,
That th'eyes of busy fools may be stopped there.
Unlace yourself, for that harmonious chime,
Tells me from you, that now it is bed time.
Off with that happy busk, which I envy,
That still can be, and still can stand so nigh.
Your gown going off, such beauteous state reveals,
As when from flowery meads th'hill's shadow steals.
Off with that wiry Coronet and shew
The hairy Diadem which on you doth grow:
Now off with those shoes, and then safely tread
In this love's hallow'd temple, this soft bed.
In such white robes, heaven's Angels used to be
Received by men; Thou Angel bringst with thee

A heaven like Mahomet's Paradise; and though
Ill spirits walk in white, we easily know,
By this these Angels from an evil sprite,
Those set our hairs, but these our flesh upright.

    Licence my roving hands, and let them go,
Before, behind, between, above, below.
O my America! my new-found-land,
My kingdom, safeliest when with one man mann'd,
My Mine of precious stones, My Empirie,
How blest am I in this discovering thee!
To enter in these bonds, is to be free;
Then where my hand is set, my seal shall be.

    Full nakedness! All joys are due to thee,
As souls unbodied, bodies uncloth'd must be,
To taste whole joys. Gems which you women use
Are like Atlanta's balls, cast in men's views,
That when a fool's eye lighteth on a Gem,
His earthly soul may covet theirs, not them.
Like pictures, or like books' gay coverings made
For lay-men, are all women thus array'd;
Themselves are mystic books, which only we
(Whom their imputed grace will dignify)
Must see reveal'd. Then since that I may know;
As liberally, as to a Midwife, shew
Thy self: cast all, yea, this white linen hence,
There is no penance due to innocence.

    To teach thee, I am naked first; why then
What needst thou have more covering than a man.

To some the poem looks like a clever verbal striptease, but it grapples with complicated ideas. Donne uses his trademark wit, especially in developing his conceits, the first of which is established in line 2: "Until I labour, I in labour lie." Bringing together two ideas in one concept, the poet refers to the labour of his erection, as well as the labour of sexual intercourse.

He goes on to establish another conceit, with further witty reference to his erection. The speaker is tired with standing and watching the enemy without engaging in battle.

His cosmic imagination is also hard at work. Urging his mistress to remove the girdle, the speaker describes it as "heaven's Zone glistering", which is the celestial sphere. Using the old cosmographic sense of space, he is favourably comparing her body ("a far fairer world") with the more ordinary sublunary sphere.

Notice how he describes her body in terms of her clothes. She merely fills the space between items of apparel: girdle, breastplate, busk, gown, coronet, shoes, white linen. The only direct reference the speaker makes to any part of her body is "the Hairy Diadem which on you doth grow". He is urging her to let her hair down and relax in the bedroom.

He says that "harmonious chime / Tells me from you, that now it is bedtime." The harmonious chime refers to time's ticking clock. When he says that it "Tells me from you", he seems to be referring to their relationship, their pending sexual union. However, perhaps he is engaging in wishful thinking – he has not yet got her into bed! Perhaps he is attempting to reach over time to the celestial sphere.

The cosmographic view of "heaven's Zone glistering" is now compared with the poet's new cosmographic view of the world.

> Licence my roving hands, and let them go,
> Before, behind, between, above, below.
> O my America! my new-found-land,

He is describing her body in cartographic view, like points on a map, bringing it to life in spatial terms as he caresses her in his imagination.

> My kingdom, safeliest when with one man mann'd,
> My mine of precious stones, My Empirie,
> How blest am I in discovering thee!

Donne is referring to the Elizabethan age of discovery as well as political changes which occurred in the seventeenth century. The need for strong political rule was significant at this time. The Renaissance had more or less put an end to the system of feudalism. The establishment of effective central government was the main political accomplishment of this period.

Calling her an angel, he is referring to the hierarchy in the Great Chain of Being – a strict hierarchical structure of all matter and life – another concept current at this time. She is bringing a heaven "like Mahomet's Paradise", which was peopled with beautiful women ready to satisfy the carnal desires of the male inhabitants.

The speaker then refers to gems (which he thinks are used by women as a means of distraction) as "Atlanta's balls". In Greek myths, Atlanta rejected all suitors who could not defeat her in a race. She was eventually defeated by Hippomenes, who dropped apples along the race course, which Atlanta stopped to pick up. The speaker is saying that women use gems as if they were "Atlanta's balls", urging her to cast off all coverings.

Let's move on to another of Donne's poems, "The Flea".

The Flea

> Mark but this flea, and mark in this,
> How little that which thou deniest me is;
> It sucked me first, and now sucks thee,
> And in this flea our two bloods mingled be;
> Thou know'st that this cannot be said
> A sin, nor shame, nor loss of maidenhead,
>   Yet this enjoys before it woo,
>   And pampered swells with one blood made of two,
>   And this, alas, is more than we would do.

Oh stay, three lives in one flea spare,
Where we almost, nay more than married are.
This flea is you and I, and this
Our marriage bed, and marriage temple is;
Though parents grudge, and you w'are met,
And cloistered in these living walls of jet.
    Though use make you apt to kill me,
    Let not to that, self-murder added be,
    And sacrilege, three sins in killing three.

Cruel and sudden, hast thou since
Purpled thy nail, in blood of innocence?
Wherein could this flea guilty be,
Except in that drop which it sucked from thee?
Yet thou triumph'st, and say'st that thou
Find'st not thy self, nor me the weaker now;
    'Tis true; then learn how false, fears be:
    Just so much honour, when thou yield'st to me,
    Will waste, as this flea's death took life from thee.

This metaphysical love poem uses the conceit of a humble flea. Through the conceit, the poet shows that, in the eyes of God and the Church, the two lovers are already conjoined because the flea has bitten both their bodies and mixed their blood.

By making reference to the sacrament of marriage, the speaker is attempting to give weight to his argument. Surrendering her virginity, he says, would be no shame under such sanctified circumstances. His argument, of course, is absurd and transparent.

The rhythm alters over the three stanzas in imitation of the sex act. In the first stanza, the tempo moves slowly when she moves to strike the flea, and he attempts to convince her of the heinous nature of this action. He contends that in killing the flea she will also be guilty of killing them both, as well as their holy union which, he argues, is embodied by the flea. She kills the flea, and its sudden death parallels sexual release.

The third stanza flows again, the rhythm similar to post-coital quietude. The speaker reflects on the fate of the flea, but then reverses his argument. Having tried to persuade her not to kill the flea – which he has claimed would mean the death of their union – he observes that the flea's death is no great matter after all. He is claiming that should she surrender her virginity they should likewise find it of no greater consequence than the death of a flea. He is trying to persuade her that any fears she may have are false.

His argument has no real substance, but the inherent contradictions are held together by the poet's wit and the internal structure of the conceit. Donne's use of conceit and metaphor is skilled and audacious. He shows great ability as a poet in embodying sexual desire, sacred love and holy marriage in a flea before turning the argument on its head.

The inconsistencies in Donne's poems reflect the inconsistencies of human behaviour. His quirks and experiences, his response to literary conventions, and his ideas about love, social relations and religion are all held together by his rhetorical wit.

Let's move on from Donne to another of the great metaphysical poets, Andrew Marvell. A masterpiece of hyperbole and metaphor, Marvell's "To His Coy Mistress" is one of the most famous love poems in the English language.

> To His Coy Mistress

> Had we but world enough, and time,
> This coyness, Lady, were no crime
> We would sit down and think which way
> To walk and pass our long love's day.
> Thou by the Indian Ganges' side
> Should'st rubies find: I by the tide
> Of Humber would complain. I would
> Love you ten years before the Flood,
> And you should, if you please, refuse
> Till the conversion of the Jews.
> My vegetable love should grow
> Vaster than empires, and more slow;
> A hundred years should go to praise
> Thine eyes and on thy forehead gaze;
> Two hundred to adore each breast,
> But thirty thousand to the rest;

An age at least to every part,
And the last age should show your heart.
For, Lady, you deserve this state,
Nor would I love at lower rate.

But at my back I always hear
Time's wingèd chariot hurrying near;
And yonder all before us lie
Deserts of vast eternity.
Thy beauty shall no more be found,
Nor, in thy marble vault, shall sound
My echoing song; then worms shall try
That long preserved virginity,
And your quaint honour turn to dust,
And into ashes all my lust:
The grave's a fine and private place,
But none, I think, do there embrace.

Now therefore, while the youthful hue
Sits on thy skin like morning dew,
And while thy willing soul transpires
At every pore with instant fires,
Now let us sport us while we may,
And now, like amorous birds of prey,
Rather at once our time devour
Than languish in his slow-chapped power.
Let us roll all our strength and all
Our sweetness up into one ball,
And tear our pleasures with rough strife

> Through the iron gates of life:
> Thus, though we cannot make our sun
> Stand still, yet we will make him run.

The poem has three verses, and each one develops the poem's argument. The basic theme of the poem is announced in the first two lines. Time lays waste to youth and life passes quickly, therefore we should enjoy our youth now and seize the day. This is a classic *carpe diem* poem.

The first verse continues to expand the theme of the first two lines. The speaker uses hyperbole (exaggeration for dramatic or rhetorical effect) when he emphasises the lovers' lack of time and space. If they had enough space and time, they could leisurely advance their courtship.

If she found rubies by the exotic River Ganges in India, he would be back in England, by the Humber River, which is slower moving by comparison. The distance between them is a metaphor for the leisurely use of time spent in praise of her.

> Thou by the Indian Ganges' side
> Should'st rubies find: I by the tide
> Of Humber would complain.

He describes the length of time it would take for him to love her, and how much time she would spend in rejecting his love. He uses the metaphor of "vegetable love", which grows very slowly but large enough to be "vaster than empire" or a great dynasty. His excessive comparisons emphasise the huge amount of time he would need to define his love for her.

> I would
> Love you ten years before the Flood,
> And you should, if you please, refuse
> Till the conversion of the Jews.

He continues to use hyperbole, overstating his beloved's physical attributes: it would take him two hundred years "to adore each breast, / But thirty thousand to the rest".

At the close of the first verse, the speaker uses a money metaphor – loving at a "certain rate" – to suggest that his beloved deserves this "state" of lavish praise because of her beauty.

The second verse shifts from vivid exaggeration to sombre images of the grave as the speaker begins to focus on the subject of death. Time is personified as a driver in a chariot: "But at my back I always here / Times' wingèd chariot hurrying near." And the image of vast deserts begins a list of comparisons related to sterility: "And yonder all before us lie / Deserts of vast eternity."

He emphasises the loss of beauty over time, implying that death is a final stopping place from where no love can escape:

> Thy beauty shall no more be found;
> Nor, in thy marble vault, shall sound
> My echoing song: then worms shall try
> That long-preserved virginity;
> And your quaint honour turn to dust
> And into ashes all my lust.

In this image the worm is penetrating her virgin corpse. "Quaint honour" suggests that virginity will be a quaint but useless treasure at the end of life. Such preserved virtues mean nothing when stretched over time.

At the close of verse two, lines 28 to 30, the poet uses understatement and irony. He praises the grave as a "fine" and "private" place. This marks a transition to the *carpe diem* argument in verse 3: "The grave's a fine and private place, / But none, I think, do there embrace." And in lines 33 and 34, the poet returns to the theme of youthful lust: "Now, therefore, while the youthful hue / Sits on thy skin like morning dew." He is insisting that the only time is now, and they should discover themselves and achieve fulfilment. He describes her young soul as breathing out "instant fires" of passion for love. There is a sense of urgency.

> And while thy willing soul transpires
> At every pore with instant fires;
> Now let us sport us while we may;

The speaker uses harsh images to lend intensity to his argument. He wants them to devour time like "amorous birds of prey", or be the victims who are slowly eaten by time. Marvell creates a frightening awareness of the inescapability of death. Time is like a predator stalking us.

He also offers a way of fighting time, which is summarised in the last two lines of the poem. Even though the lovers cannot command time to "stand still", time cannot control their love: "Thus, though we cannot make our sun / Stand still, yet we will make him run."

ROBERT BURNS

Robert Burns (1759–1796) was Scotland's national poet. His birthday, known as Burns Night, is still celebrated around the world. After Queen Victoria and Christopher Columbus, Robert Burns has more statues dedicated to him than any other non-religious figure. There are statues and memorials in Scotland, England, Canada, Australia, and New Zealand. Sixty years ago, a translation of "My Hearts in the Highlands" was adopted as the marching song of the Chinese resistance fighters in the Second World War. Burns fathered many children, some of them illegitimate. On the day of his funeral when he was aged 37, his wife gave birth to their nineteenth child.

Burns's poetic style is marked by spontaneity, directness and sincerity. Scottish novelist Andrew O'Hagan states that Burns has "an uncanny connection with people's cares and wishes for a better life." He also says that Burns has "a quality of empathy that radiates from everything that touched his imagination."

Burns has had a major influence on other poets, including William Wordsworth and Samuel Taylor Coleridge. Nobel Laureate Bob Dylan has said that his greatest creative inspiration is not Woody Guthrie but this eighteenth-century poet known to many as Rabbie Burns. Dylan named Burns's "A Red Red Rose" as the poem which had the greatest impact on his life. Let's take a look at it.

<u>A Red Red Rose</u>

O my Luve is like a red, red rose
    That's newly sprung in June;
O my Luve is like the melody
    That's sweetly played in tune.

So fair art thou, my bonnie lass,
    So deep in luve am I;
And I will luve thee still, my dear,
    Till a' the seas gang dry.

Till a' the seas gang dry, my dear,
    And the rocks melt wi' the sun;
I will love thee still, my dear,
    While the sands o' life shall run.

And fare thee weel, my only luve!
    And fare thee weel awhile!
And I will come again, my luve,
    Though it were ten thousand mile.

In "A Red Red Rose" Burns uses a conventional conceit – a woman is compared to a flower. The rose is "newly sprung", perfect and pure, its vitality and freshness intact, not yet faded. But the rose is a temporary embodiment of love. The lines "my Luve's like the melodie / That's sweetly played in tune" refer to the transience of beauty. Remember, of course, that there was no means of recording music when this poem was written.

He also compares his beloved to divine song, lifting the subject matter above moral concerns of time and space. A series of similes flows from one image into the next, building an argument, picture by picture, to form a wonderful addition to the tradition of love poetry. The poem is also a subtle meditation on the consciousness of time, as it seeks to strike a balance between the temporal and the eternal. And the direct reference to time ("While all the sands o' life shall run") reminds us of the first two lines of the poem, with the time-bound state of the rose.

The use of quatrains (four line stanzas) gives the poem a wonderful sense of song. Using the evocative "O", the speaker is calling on the Muses for assistance. By comparing the beloved to divine song, the poet lifts the subject matter above the mortal concerns of time and space. His love will outlast the timespan of the seas, and will be stronger than any geographical distance that may become between them.

In the final stanza, the poem turns from the consciousness of time to that of parting. The speaker will transcend not only vast distance ("ten thousand miles") but also time itself:

> And fare thee weel, my only luve!
>   And fare thee weel awhile!
> And I will come again, my luve,
>   Though it were ten thousand mile.

ELIZABETH BARRETT BROWNING

Elizabeth Barrett Browning (1806–1861) was one of the most prominent and successful poets of her time. During her lifetime she was even more popular than her husband, fellow poet Robert Browning. Elizabeth's father had forbidden any of his children to marry, wishing them to remain dependent on him, so in 1846 Robert and Elizabeth married secretly. Immediately after the marriage, the couple left for the warmer climate of Italy in order to protect Elizabeth's frail health. She remained in Italy till her death. Despite the responsibilities of marriage and motherhood – their only child, Robert Weidemann Barrett Browning, known as "Pen", was born in 1849 – she was determined to pursue her literary career.

"How Do I Love Thee? Let me Count the Ways" is one of the most recognisable poems in the English language. It is Sonnet 43 in a series, *Sonnets from the Portuguese,* written by

Barrett Browning for her husband. She published these poems as if they were translations from the Portuguese in order to fully express her feelings and to save them both from embarrassment. "My little Portuguese" was Robert's nickname for his wife. She kept the forty-four sonnets in a notebook, and showed them to her husband in 1849. He insisted that they appear in her forthcoming edition of *Poems,* published in 1850.

How Do I Love Thee? Let Me Count the Ways

> How do I love thee? Let me count the ways.
> I love thee to the depth and breadth and height
> My soul can reach, when feeling out of sight
> For the ends of being and ideal grace.
> I love thee to the level of every day's
> Most quiet need, by sun and candle-light.
> I love thee freely, as men strive for right.
> I love thee purely, as they turn from praise.
> I love thee with the passion put to use
> In my old griefs, and with my childhood's faith.
> I love thee with a love I seemed to lose
> With my lost saints. I love thee with the breath,
> Smiles, tears, of all my life; and, if God choose,
> I shall but love thee better after death.

The poem recalls the sonnets of Shakespeare we read earlier, though this is not a strict Shakespearean sonnet. Instead it adapts and develops the form. It is classified as a sonnet because it has 14 lines, it has a fixed line scheme of ABBA ABBA CDCD CD, and it is written in iambic pentameter (di *dum* di *dum* di *dum* di *dum*, di *dum*). Below, the arrows mark the beats.

```
   v     v      v       v      v
```
How do I love thee? Let me count the ways.

The speaker begins by posing the question "How do I love thee?" and then goes on to count the ways. Although Elizabeth is expressing her love for her husband, this poem is not gender specific; it works if the speaker is considered male or female.

In lines 2 to 4, the poet uses a spatial metaphor:

> I love thee to the depth and breadth and height
> My soul can reach, when feeling out of sight
> For the ends of being and ideal grace.

She is feeling for the edges of her "being" that are just out of sight, and she realises that her love extends just as far as her soul extends in the world. Internal rhyme ("feeling", "being") binds the poem together.

In lines 5 to 6, she loves her beloved "to the level of everyday's / Most quiet need". This gives a sense of everyday domestic living. And in lines 7 and 8, the speaker says "I love thee freely, as men strive for right. / I love thee purely, as they turn from praise." As those men who strive to be morally good, choosing freely to do so, she makes the choice freely to love her husband. And she loves him "purely", not expecting praise for it; it is just something she has to do.

In lines 9 and 10, the passion of "old griefs" is transformed into the passion of love. And in lines 11 and 12 she loves "with a love I seemed to lose / With my lost saints". This is the kind of love you have had for your heroes in the past, but you no longer invest in them the same degree of faith.

In lines 12 and 13, she loves him with the "breath / Smiles, tears, of all my life." She loves him with every emotion, each one an expression of her love for him. Even the breaths she takes are expressions of her love. In the final lines, the speaker says that if God allows her, she will love him even more intensely after death:

> I love thee with the breath,
> Smiles, tears, of all my life; and if God choose,
> I shall love thee better after death.

ROBERT BROWNING

Robert Browning (1812–1889) was a preeminent Victorian poet. He was a prolific writer, and wrote plays as well as poetry, but he is now best known for his dramatic monologues. He is considered a master of portraying the dramatic situation in poetry. Oscar Wilde commented in his essay "The Critic as Artist" that Browning's "sense of dramatic situation was unrivalled". Browning's poems are also known for their irony, rich characterisation, dark humour, cutting social commentary, historical settings, and challenging vocabulary and syntax. His poem "Love Among the Ruins" was published in his 1855 collection *Men and Women*.

Love Among the Ruins

Where the quiet-coloured end of evening smiles,
    Miles and miles
On the solitary pastures where our sheep
    Half-asleep

Tinkle homeward thro' the twilight, stray or stop
    As they crop—
Was the site once of a city great and gay,
    (So they say)
Of our country's very capital, its prince
    Ages since
Held his court in, gathered councils, wielding far
    Peace or war.

Now the country does not even boast a tree,
    As you see,
To distinguish slopes of verdure, certain rills
    From the hills
Intersect and give a name to, (else they run
    Into one)
Where the domed and daring palace shot its spires
    Up like fires
O'er the hundred-gated circuit of a wall
    Bounding all
Made of marble, men might march on nor be prest
    Twelve abreast.

And such plenty and perfection, see, of grass
    Never was!
Such a carpet as, this summer-time, o'er-spreads
    And embeds
Every vestige of the city, guessed alone,
    Stock or stone—

Where a multitude of men breathed joy and woe
    Long ago;
Lust of glory pricked their hearts up, dread of shame
    Struck them tame;
And that glory and that shame alike, the gold
    Bought and sold.

Now—the single little turret that remains
    On the plains,
By the caper overrooted, by the gourd
    Overscored,
While the patching houseleek's head of blossom winks
    Through the chinks—
Marks the basement whence a tower in ancient time
    Sprang sublime,
And a burning ring, all round, the chariots traced
    As they raced,
And the monarch and his minions and his dames
    Viewed the games.

And I know, while thus the quiet-coloured eve
    Smiles to leave
To their folding, all our many-tinkling fleece
    In such peace,
And the slopes and rills in undistinguished grey
    Melt away—
That a girl with eager eyes and yellow hair
    Waits me there

In the turret whence the charioteers caught soul
    For the goal,
When the king looked, where she looks now, breathless, dumb
    Till I come.

But he looked upon the city, every side,
    Far and wide,
All the mountains topped with temples, all the glades'
    Colonnades,
All the causeys, bridges, aqueducts,—and then
    All the men!
When I do come, she will speak not, she will stand,
    Either hand
On my shoulder, give her eyes the first embrace
    Of my face,
Ere we rush, ere we extinguish sight and speech
    Each on each.

In one year they sent a million fighters forth
    South and North,
And they built their gods a brazen pillar high
    As the sky
Yet reserved a thousand chariots in full force—
    Gold, of course.
O heart! oh blood that freezes, blood that burns!
    Earth's returns
For whole centuries of folly, noise and sin!
    Shut them in,

> With their triumphs and their glories and the rest!
> Love is best.

While gazing on a rural landscape, the site of an ancient and ruined city, the poem's speaker makes a statement about the value of love. Browning combines several techniques. The first is contrast. He creates contrasts between excitement and serenity, city and pastoral, past and present, girl (the speaker's beloved) and king, love and power, heroic glory and rural tranquillity. The "solitary" (unfrequented) pastures were "the site once of a city great and gay." This was the "country's very capital" where the "prince / Ages since / Held his court" and "wielded … / Peace or war." The speaker describes the city "where the domed and daring palace shot its spires / Up like fires." But the green vegetation ("verdure") has overtaken the city. The past city did not have the present "plenty and perfection" of the grass, "this summer-time" growth which "o'erspreads / And embeds / Every vestige of the city."

Browning employs an unusual line structure, pairing long trochaic lines (*di* dum *di* dum *di* dum) with short lines of three syllables. The short lines provide an echo to the longer lines. He also uses a variable rhythm. He uses a slow, quiet rhythm to describe the state of tranquillity (the houseleek "winks / Through the chinks" of the crumbled walls of the "single little turret"). But he uses a faster rhythm to describe the "multitude of men" breathing "joy and woe" or pricking up their hearts with "lust of glory." These clamorous crowds of men have strong emotions, which contrasts with the "breathless, dumb" demeanour of his beloved. The speaker recalls the "burning ring" where "the chariots traced / As they raced" , again with quick rhythm. In stanza four, the speaker draws our attention to the "girl with eager eyes and yellow hair" who is waiting for him in the turret "whence the charioteers caught soul / For the goal." Again, a slower and quieter rhythm.

The poet shifts the poem's focus throughout the seven stanzas. The speaker returns to his description of the once-great city where "they built their gods a brazen pillar high / As the sky", and where they "reserved a thousand chariots in full force." And the speaker is struck with awe at the city's past glory: "Oh, heart! oh, blood that freezes, blood that burns." But he determines to "shut in" all those centuries of "folly, noise and sin!" He prefers to embrace his beloved: "Love is best."

CHRISTINA ROSSETTI

Christina Rossetti (1830–1894) wrote poems about the impossibility of fulfilling love. They express frustration at the inadequacy of a physical, mutable world to adequately contain something like immortal love. They capture the intensity of her feelings and emotions with painful precision. Philip Larkin said that Rossetti's work "is unequalled for its objective expression of happiness denied and a certain unfamiliar, steely stoicism." Rossetti's "Dream-Love" is a good example.

Dream-Love

Young Love lies sleeping
    In May-time of the year,
Among the lilies,
    Lapped in the tender light:
White lambs come grazing,
    White doves come building there;
And round about him
    The May-bushes are white.

Soft moss the pillow
    For oh, a softer cheek;
Broad leaves cast shadow
    Upon the heavy eyes:
There winds and waters
    Grow lulled and scarcely speak;
There twilight lingers
    The longest in the skies.

Young Love lies dreaming;
    But who shall tell the dream?
A perfect sunlight
    On rustling forest tips;
Or perfect moonlight
    Upon a rippling stream;
Or perfect silence,
    Or song of cherished lips.

Burn odours round him
    To fill the drowsy air;
Weave silent dances
    Around him to and fro;
For oh, in waking
    The sights are not so fair,
And song and silence
    Are not like these below.

Young Love lies dreaming
    Till summer days are gone,—

Dreaming and drowsing
   Away to perfect sleep:
He sees the beauty
   Sun hath not looked upon,
And tastes the fountain
   Unutterably deep.

Him perfect music
   Doth hush unto his rest,
And through the pauses
   The perfect silence calms:
Oh, poor the voices
   Of earth from east to west,
And poor earth's stillness
   Between her stately palms.

Young Love lies drowsing
   Away to poppied death;
Cool shadows deepen
   Across the sleeping face:
So fails the summer
   With warm, delicious breath;
And what hath autumn
   To give us in its place?

Draw close the curtains
   Of branched evergreen;
Change cannot touch them
   With fading fingers sere:

> Here the first violets
>   Perhaps will bud unseen,
> And a dove, may be,
>   Return to nestle here.

"Dream-Love" depicts a figure sleeping and dreaming in a natural landscape. The sleeper is a metaphor for young love itself. He is withdrawn and isolated, oblivious to "the month of nature's passion and fulfilment." He does not see the white doves building their nests for procreation: "Young love lies dreaming; / But who shall tell the dream?"

He is isolated from the world, with his perfect silence, perfect music and perfect sleep. In his isolation he "sees the beauty / Sun hath not looked upon." If he wakes, "the sights are not so fair." Nature remains unseen.

Here is another Rossetti poem, "A Birthday." On the surface, the poem appears optimistic. It is one of Rossetti's more sanguine poems about love. But a closer reading reveals that the possibility of attaining love is ultimately suspect.

<u>A Birthday</u>

> My heart is like a singing bird
>   Whose nest is in a water'd shoot;
> My heart is like an apple-tree
>   Whose boughs are bent with thickset fruit;

My heart is like a rainbow shell
    That paddles in a halcyon sea;
My heart is gladder than all these
    Because my love is come to me.
Raise me a dais of silk and down;
    Hang it with vair and purple dyes;
Carve it in doves and pomegranates,
    And peacocks with a hundred eyes;
Work it in gold and silver grapes,
    In leaves and silver fleurs-de-lys;
Because the birthday of my life
    Is come, my love is come to me.

In the first stanza, the speaker uses precisely drawn natural details to describe her heart and her expectations. These images from nature are lush and exuberant, suggesting ripeness and fecundity. Her heart "is like a singing bird / Whose nest is in a water'd shoot." This suggests the idea of having a family with her beloved, but it also carries a suggestion of dangerous water turbulence. Her heart is "like an apple-tree" laden with "thick-set fruit": the very ripe fruit, subject to nature, may be about to drop off the tree. Her heart is "like a rainbow shell on a halcyon sea": this moment of calm is subject to change when the sea becomes rough. Her heart is "gladder than all these / Because my love is come to me."

The poem shifts in the second stanza from describing happiness in her heart as the speaker orders preparations for the elaborate ceremonial celebration of "the birthday in my life" because "my love is come to me." Like the first stanza, the images are exuberant and luxurious, but they are also somewhat gaudy and grandiose. Plush luxuriance associated with royalty is suggested by a "dais of silk and down," as well as "purple dyes" and "silver fleurs-de-lys" (both associated with royalty). The speaker wants doves, pomegranates and peacocks carved into the royal platform, along with "gold and silver grapes."

The elements of the dais are not natural; they are manufactured representations of nature. The "vair" (squirrel fur) and down come from dead animals. The birds and fruit are carved in wood: they have a longer life than the buds and fruit of the first stanza, but they are static imitations. Thus they suggest the betrayal of the speaker's expectations and the impossibility of attaining fulfilment.

Let's look at another Rossetti poem.

A Triad

> Three sang of love together: one with lips
>   Crimson, with cheeks and bosom in a glow,
> Flushed to the yellow hair and finger tips;
>   And one there sang who soft and smooth as snow
>   Bloomed like a tinted hyacinth at a show;
> And one was blue with famine after love,
>   Who like a harpstring snapped rang harsh and low
> The burden of what those were singing of.

> One shamed herself in love; one temperately
>   Grew gross in soulless love, a sluggish wife;
> One famished died for love. Thus two of three
>   Took death for love and won him after strife;
> One droned in sweetness like a fattened bee:
>   All on the threshold, yet all short of life.

"A Triad" portrays three types of female passion, all three of them failing to reach fulfilment. It parodies the Petrarchan sonnet form, which traditionally idealises love.

The first woman singing about love is preoccupied with the pursuit of sensual pleasure. Heavily made up "with crimson lips", she conveys a ready voluptuousness, with "cheeks and bosoms in a glow" and "Flushed to the yellow hair and finger tips." Having shamed herself in love, she "droned in sweetness like a fattened bee." The monotony of her bee-like humming does not convey a sense of joy or fulfilment. A drone is, after all, a male bee that produces no honey.

The second woman, "soft and smooth as snow", looks cool and enticing but is cold to the touch. She "blooms like a tinted hyacinth at a show." Beguiling and disingenuous, she is prepared to settle for too little, lacking in energy to be anything more than "a sluggish wife."

After experiencing love, the third woman is left "blue with famine." Starved now of love's oxygen, she is like "a harpstring snapped", singing a harsh note, remaining unfulfilled.

While the first woman is "droning [...] like a fattened bee", the second and third women opt for a living death "won after strife" – a prize not worth fighting for. All three women are "on the threshold" but are doomed to be "short of life."

Let's move on to look at another poem.

<u>When I am dead, my dearest</u>

When I am dead, my dearest,
    Sing no sad songs for me;
Plant thou no roses at my head,
    Nor shady cypress tree:
Be the green grass above me
    With showers and dewdrops wet;
And if thou wilt, remember,
    And if thou wilt, forget.

I shall not see the shadows,
    I shall not feel the rain;
I shall not hear the nightingale
    Sing on, as if in pain:
And dreaming through the twilight
    That doth not rise nor set,
Haply I may remember,
    And haply may forget.

Christina Rossetti wrote this poem in 1848, when she was still a teenager. It was published in 1862, in her first volume of poetry, "Goblin Market and Other Poems." It seems to be a simple song on first reading, but it has complex implications.

In the first stanza the speaker asks her beloved not to sing any sad songs for her, or put flowers or plant a tree on her grave. The grass on the grave, showered by rain and morning dew, will be enough. She permits him to choose freely ("if thou wilt") between remembering and forgetting. Thus she relieves him of the widow's duty to grieve.

In the second stanza she explains why she is not concerned about whether or not her beloved remembers her when she is dead. She will no longer see the shadows or feel the rain, or hear the nightingale singing. After death she will be "dreaming" and sleeping through a "twilight". She may remember him, or she may not. Thus she releases herself, but from what? From the pain of living, perhaps. Or the pain of inadequate earthly love. Perhaps she will no longer feel desire for him.

One last poem from Rossetti before we move on.

Remember

Remember me when I am gone away,
    Gone far away into the silent land;
    When you can no more hold me by the hand,
Nor I half turn to go yet turning stay.

> Remember me when no more day by day
>   You tell me of our future that you plann'd:
>   Only remember me; you understand
> It will be late to counsel then or pray.
> Yet if you should forget me for a while
>   And afterwards remember, do not grieve:
>   For if the darkness and corruption leave
>   A vestige of the thoughts that once I had,
> Better by far you should forget and smile
>   Than that you should remember and be sad.

This is another poem which appears to be fairly simple on first reading, but which on closer inspection is not straightforward.

The speaker asks her beloved to remember her "when I am gone away / Gone far away." The repetition here reinforces the distance that will exist between them when she is gone. When she dies she will go to "the silent land" where there is no communication: "when no more day by day / You tell me of our future that you plann'd". And there will be no more closeness, no physical contact: "When you can no more hold me by the hand, / Nor I half turn to go yet turning stay." It will be "too late to counsel then or pray". That is, there will be no more consultation or spiritual hoping. Then comes the turn or volta in the sonnet's sestet.

> Yet if you should forget me for a while
>   And afterwards remember, do not grieve:

She would prefer that he remember her completely and eternally. If there is a "vestige" (a trace) of her "thoughts", she would prefer him to "forget and smile" rather than "remember and be sad." But this is ambiguous. After all, does she want to be remembered at all? How would her thoughts leave any trace except in his thoughts?

W.H. AUDEN

W.H. Auden wrote many poems about love. He used striking imagery and hyperbole as well as extended metaphor, and he gave freshness to the theme of love. "Stop All the Clocks" is a poem about the death of a loved one, and the speaker's grief.

<u>Stop All the Clocks</u>

"Stop All the Clocks", also known as "Funeral Blues", can be read by searching on the internet for "W H Auden Stop All the Clocks".

The first two stanzas are made up of a series of requests from the speaker concerning preparations for a funeral. There is a formal tone and a mournful mood, but the opening stanzas do not express personal grief or sadness. The imagery conveys the speaker's determined attitude, a recognition of duty to the dead, of the need for procedure and proper action, reflecting the expectations of society. "Stop the clocks" is not a figure of speech. It is an old formal custom to turn off the clocks, as it was thought bad luck to have them working with a dead person present. And the "muffled drum" even today is still a traditional custom at military funerals.

In the second stanza, there is a continuation of the preparations made in the first stanza. However, the requests are full of hyperbole.

But in the third stanza there is a move in the poem to a more striking depiction and outpouring of grief, using hyperbole. It is revealed that the deceased must have some close and personal connection to the speaker. In the ninth line, the underlying tensions are revealed, and we see how utterly bereaved the speaker is: "He was my North, my South, my East and my West". This line conveys the loss of life direction one feels when someone close to us dies. There is a sense that no matter what happens, the grief is too big for any funeral to adequately cover it.

In the fourth stanza there is an even greater outpouring of emotion. The stars are used as a metaphor for aspirations which guide us through life. The moon and the sun are imagery for the heart and mind. And the ocean conveys a depth of feeling.

This beautiful poem was given a fresh audience when it was featured in the 1994 British romantic comedy *Four Weddings and a Funeral*. It is read by Mathew (John Hannah) as he mourns the death of his partner, Gareth (Simon Callow). You can view John Hannah's reading by searching on the internet for "John Hannah Stop all the Clocks".

The More Loving One

Let's look at another of Auden's great love poems. You can read this poem by searching on the internet for "W H Auden The Move Loving One."

This poem uses an extended metaphor to express the speaker's feelings about an unrequited love. The stars in the metaphor represent lovers who do not feel the same about the human who loves them. We don't usually think of stars as lovers, but even today, with astrology scientifically discredited, we often think about the celestial in relation to fate and fortune. Despite modern scientific understanding, stars are still great mysteries. It is an apt metaphor for unrequited love because, like a lover, the stars are both familiar and alien, seemingly close yet unthinkably far away.

The extended metaphor is established in the first two lines of the first stanza. The speaker finds that his love is not returned, and that the lover is indifferent. However, perhaps he would prefer the lover to be indifferent rather than show hatred or be vulnerable to a love that goes unrequited by him. This theme continues into the second stanza, when the speaker says it is better to be the one who loves.

The tone shifts a little in the third stanza. The speaker recognises that the love he feels is fleeting and impermanent. He sees that the stars "do not give a damn". But in the fourth stanza, he contemplates how he would feel if all the stars were to disappear or die. He would "learn to look at an empty sky / And feel its total dark sublime." But it "might take me a little time." He says that he would recover from such a complete loss in the course of time.

O Tell Me the Truth about Love

You can read this poem on the internet by searching for "W H Auden O Tell Me the Truth About Love".

In this poem Auden skilfully and playfully considers the nature and form of love. As he confirms our everyday experiences with familiar but new images, he gives stunning freshness to the subject. This makes the poem easily and immediately accessible to the reader. Some of this freshness also comes from his avoidance of sentimentality.

Auden relates the subject of love to everyday details using humour, wit and absurdity. What is love? he asks throughout the poem. Is it a little boy or a bird? He even asked the man next door. What does it sound or smell like?

What is its texture? He suggests places where it might be found, such as Brighton or Maidenhead, in the summerhouse or at the races. Or will it "come without warning / Just as I am picking my nose?"

Why do we connect to this poem so readily? Why does it resonate with us with such immediacy? Apart from the few characters in the first stanza, Auden has shifted the focus on love from human interaction to ordinary daily objects (pianos, beds, chicken-runs, et cetera) and activities (pulling faces, fiddling with string). We don't usually think about love in this way; Auden gives us an unusual and new perspective. But the idea of love, and our feelings associated with it, permeate our lives completely and permanently, and in every aspect. Auden draws our attention to this. Perhaps the poem also reflects something of the varied aspects of our character, as individuals and as a culture.

Here's another poem by Auden.

<u>Lullaby</u>

You can read this poem by searching on the internet for "W H Auden Lullaby".

This poem is both an unconventional love poem and an unconventional lullaby. A lullaby is usually sung by a parent (typically the mother) to a child, and is intended to put the child to sleep. Its focus is not normally an already sleeping lover, as it is in this poem.

Most love poems take the romantic view that love makes us better than we are. But here the speaker describes himself from the beginning as faithless. There is no promise of a lasting relationship, as certainty and fidelity "On the stroke of midnight pass." The poem is a celebration of physical love in spite of its ephemerality, in spite of human unfaithfulness, and in spite of its toll on the wallet. Recognising love's imperfections, the speaker decides to live for the moment, watching his lover who is "the entirely beautiful." Although it is temporary and casual, the moment will be remembered:

> Not a whisper, not a thought,
> Nor a kiss nor a look be lost.

The ecstasy of their physical union will lead to the lovers' spiritual communion, as "Soul and body have no bounds." Venus sends a "grave" vision of "supernatural sympathy / Universal love and hope". That is, individual love can lead to the love of humanity. The physical union of the lovers is as valuable as the "abstract insight" of the hermit which leads to his "carnal ecstasy."

The speaker hopes that his lover will be able to live fully in spite of the imperfections of life, that he will be able to withstand the "Noons of dryness" and be fed by "involuntary powers", the spontaneous actions of others.

There is a sense of time passing and things coming to an end, yet something remains. What is important is the moment – it is intense and it will live in the memory.

BOB DYLAN

Bob Dylan's love songs are more than songs and about more than love. With his fusion of poetry with traditional or popular American music, he has helped restore the ancient link between poetry and music. As he has said, his lyrics "are meant to be sung, not read." Dylan "is without a doubt the finest artist using this oral form of creation in the English language today.' He was rejecting the popular music of the time and providing a "freshness and honesty." (Dr Bill King.)

Let me begin with a brief personal recollection. When I was a teenager in the 1960s, Bob Dylan burst onto the popular music scene with his poetic lyrics. At my school's Talent Night in 1964 I sang "Blowing in the Wind" with a small group of girls. I was only thirteen years old and Dylan seemed much older. But he was really just a skinny white Jewish kid from the American Mid-West, in his early twenties, who had a clear vision and enormous talent. As he said in his acceptance speech for the 2016 Nobel Prize for

Literature, "I wanted to write songs unlike anything anybody ever heard."

<u>I Want You</u>

The lyrics of "I Want You" can be read on the internet by searching for "Bob Dylan I Want You". A video of Dylan singing the song can be viewed on the internet by searching for "Bob Dylan I Want You" on YouTube.

As with many of Dylan's love songs, "I Want You" is not just about love. Dr Bill King describes it as Dylan's "finest rebuttal of what he calls the 'True Love' myth". And he goes on to explain what he means by social myth:

> It is the mid-twentieth-century American social myth of love that is pure and sexless. It is eternal and never fades away [...] This kind of vapidity, of falseness, permeated popular music up into the sixties. It conveys a naïve and even phony attitude toward love still apparent in early Beatles songs: "I Want to Hold Your Hand."

In "I Want You" Dylan gives an assessment of traditional sappy love songs. He is also saying something about his own role in the American popular music tradition. The verses describe the obstacles to fulfilment, while the chorus is a simple expression of desire, with no sentimental metaphors.

In the first verse, the "guilty undertaker sighs" with the weariness of dealing with death, as well as perhaps his own feeling of unfulfillment. The "silver saxophones and washed out horns" blowing into Dylan's face with scorn suggest contempt for anyone who fails to live up to the empty dream. The "cracked bells" suggest the false view of love as well as disillusionment.

The line "I wasn't born to lose you" suggests, according to Dr Bill King, the life cycle in reverse order. It goes back to the "guilty undertaker" (King). It is reminiscent of a line in Samuel Beckett's play *Waiting for Godot*: "We give birth astride the grave." This has a similar telescoping effect on birth and death. Dylan is warning us not to live as if we are born astride the grave. It's important to live life properly. We are not born only to die without experiencing life.

The second verse emphasises the link between the phony idea of true love with the phoniness of politics and religion. Drunken politicians, weeping mothers and sleeping saviours – all preach the same false views: "And I wait for them to interrupt / My drinkin' from my broken cup."

The cup is an image traditionally associated with the positive living of life: "My cup runneth over" is the translation from Hebrew in the King James Version of the Holy Bible. The phrase also appears in Psalm 23, and it figures prominently in modern music, used in Broadway musicals, by rappers, rock musicians, and in TV shows and movies. Dylan's "broken cup" suggests the difficulty of finding fulfilment in a phony world.

Fathers and daughters subscribe to the false myth but have "gone down" with all the others. The daughters put him down because he won't give it a thought.

So he returns to the Queen of Spades. This refers to the song "The Little Queen of Spades" by the black American blues singer Robert Johnson. The speaker talks with the chambermaid who, in her lowly position, has more wisdom and acceptance than the drunken politicians and weeping mothers. He is "not afraid to look at her" and see things differently.

According to Dr Bill King, the "dancing child with his Chinese suit" could be an image of modern popular music. Or perhaps it refers to someone who is too young to be fully aware of the false myth, and who is dancing to the tune of the purveyors of the myth while wearing clothes which are foreign imports. "I wasn't very cute to him", says Dylan, as he takes the dancing child's flute – that is, he takes up the music, the song, from those who would sell him their phony attitudes. He also takes the flute because "time was on his [the child's] side." Note that he says that time *was* on his side, suggesting that Dylan's aspiration contains much more hope.

GLOSSARY OF KEY LITERARY TERMS

CARPE DIEM

"Carpe" is derived from the Latin word for "pick" or "pluck". In his "Odes", written in 23 BC, Horace used it to mean "to enjoy, seize, make use of." "Diem" comes from the Latin word "dies", which means "day". So a literal translation of "carpe diem" would mean "seize the day." Andrew Marvell's poem, "To His Coy Mistress", is perhaps the most famous *carpe diem* poem in the English language. Another good example is the poem, "To the Virgins, to Make Much of Time", written by Robert Herrick (1591 – 1674). It begins:

> Gather ye rose-buds while ye may,
> Old Time is a-flying;
> And this same flower that smiles today
> Tomorrow will be dying.

The idea of *carpe diem* is featured in the movie, *Dead Poets Society* (1989). The English teacher John Keating – played by Robin Williams – says to the boys in his class, "Carpe diem. Seize the day, boys. Make your lives extraordinary."

COUPLET

A couplet consists of two successive lines that rhyme and have the same meter. A good example of a rhyming couplet, which is one of the simplest rhyme schemes in poetry, is found in a poem by John Donne, "Love's Alchemy":

So, lovers dream a rich and long delight,
But get a winter-seeming summer's night.

DRAMATIC MONOLOGUE

A dramatic monologue is a type of poem written in the form of a speech given by an individual character. One of the most famous poems written in the form of a dramatic monologue is Robert Browning's "My Last Duchess."

HYPERBOLE

Derived from the Greek word for "overshooting", hyperbole is a deliberately bold overstatement of extravagant exaggeration of fact, not usually meant to be taken literally. We often use hyperbole in everyday speech. For example, "I have a ton of chores to do."

IRONY

Irony is a literary technique in which what appears on the surface, to be the case, differs greatly from what actually is the case. In the ancient Greek theatre, the *eiron* was one of three stock characters in comedy. A clever underdog and a dissembler, the *eiron* characteristically pretended to be less clever than he was, and usually succeeded in bringing down his braggart opponent, the *alazon*, by understating his abilities. Irony also derives from the Latin word, *ironia*.

LYRIC

In Ancient Greece the lyric was a song accompanied by a lyre, a stringed instrument. We now think of a lyric as a poem which is usually short in length, and expressing personal thoughts and emotions without the plot and character development common to narrative and epic poetry. Lyric poems do not require rhyme or regular meter, although many do rhyme. Some of the best known songs of all time are lyric poems that were set to music, such as "Auld Lang Syne" by Robert Burns or the traditional song, "Greensleeves." Lyric was the dominant poetic form in seventeenth poetry from John Donne to Andrew Marvell. In Europe the lyric was also the principal poetic form during the nineteenth century. Romantic lyric poetry consists of first person accounts of the thoughts and feelings of a specific moment, the feelings are extreme and often intensely personal. Some of the greatest lyric poets of this time were Samuel Taylor Coleridge, Percy Bysshe Shelley and Lord Byron. During the Victorian era, Robert Browning and Christina Rossetti were two main poets writing in the lyric form. In the twentieth century, lyric poetry continued as a dominant form of poetry in the US, Britain and the British colonies. But with the advance of modernism, the growing mechanisation of society, and the harsh realities of war, the relevance and acceptance of lyric poetry was called into question by some leading poets, such as T S Eliot. Some of the most well known contemporary songwriters are lyric poets. Bob Dylan and Paul Simon are some good examples.

METER

We naturally speak English with rhythm –that is, in a recognisable but varied pattern in the beat of the stresses in the stream of sound. When this rhythm is structured into recurrent, regular, approximately equal units, we call it meter. It gives poetry a rhythmical and melodious sound. What makes meter in a poem is the pattern of stressed and unstressed syllables. These patterns are defined in groupings, called feet, of two or three syllables.

An iamb is a type of foot which consists of one unstressed syllable followed by a stressed syllable. e.g. reWARD, in CASE. A trochee, another type of foot, consists of a stressed syllable followed by an unstressed syllable. e.g. CARRiage, UPside.

These types of feet are further classified into the number of feet in each line. For instance, a line in tetrameter has four feet. And a line in pentameter has five feet.

Accordingly, a line of verse in iambic pentameter has five iambs in each line. That is, di *dum*, di *dum*, di *dum*, di *dum*, di *dum*.

And a line of verse in trochaic pentameter has five trochees. That is *dum* di, *dum* di, *dum* di, *dum* di, *dum* di. The iambic pentameter is the most commonly used meter in English verse.

METAPHOR

A metaphor is a figure of speech that describes an object, quality or action in a way that is not literally true, but helps to explain an idea or make a comparison. A metaphor states that one thing *is* another thing, and equates these two things not because they are actually the same, but for the sake of comparison or symbolism. We use metaphor frequently in everyday speed eg. That suitcase weighed a ton.

PASTORAL

In a pastoral poem, the urban poet expresses nostalgia for the peace and simplicity of the life of shepherds and other rural folk in an idealised natural setting. "Pastor" is Latin for "shepherd". The first pastoral poems were written by Theocritus in the third century BC.

Renaissance writers in English used the pastoral in various literary forms. Sir Philip Sidney's "Arcadia" is a long pastoral romance written in elaborate prose. Arcadia was a mountainous region in Greece which represented Sidney's idealised pastoral vision.

Christopher Marlowe's "The Passionate Shepherd to his Love" is one of the most famous pastoral lyrics written in English.

In 1590 Edmund Spenser wrote "The Faerie Queene" in honour of Queen Elizabeth I. It is a very famous pastoral epic which employs the pastoral mode to accentuate the charm, lushness and splendour of the poem's natural world.

John Milton's "Paradise Lost" is another very famous pastoral epic, featuring Adam and Eve's pastorally idyllic, eternally fertile living conditions.

QUATRAIN

A quatrain is a type of stanza in a poem, or a complete poem of four lines. There are 15 possible rhyme schemes but the most common are: AAAA. ABAB, ABBA.

OCTAVE

Octave has been derived from the Latin word *octāva*, which means "eighth part." It is a type of verse that contains eight lines, which usually appear in an iambic pentameter. In simple words, it can be any stanza in a poem that has eight lines and follows a rhymed or unrhymed meter.

SONNET

A sonnet is a lyric poem written in a single stanza, and consisting of 14 iambic pentameter lines linked by an intricate rhyme scheme. There are two main types of sonnet written in English. The Italian or Petrarchan sonnet has two main parts: an octave of eight lines, rhyming ABBAABBA and a sestet of six lines, usually rhyming CDECDE. There is often a statement of a problem, situation or incident in the octave, with a resolution in the sestet. An English or Shakespearean sonnet has three quatrains and a concluding couplet. Its rhyme scheme is ABABCDCDEFEFGG. The rhyme scheme and structure of the Shakespearean sonnet work together to emphasise the idea of the poem. Both Petrarch and Shakespeare used the structure of the sonnet to explore the multiple facets of a theme in a short piece.

STANZA

A stanza is a grouped set of lines within a poem, usually set off from other stanzas by a blank line or indentation. Stanzas can have regular rhyme and metrical schemes, although they are not required to have either. There are many unique forms of stanza. Some are simple, such as four line quatrains. The stanza in poetry is analogous with the paragraph in prose. Related thoughts are grouped into units.

REFERENCES

"About the poems of Christina Rosetti." *British Library: Learning Poetry and Performance.* Web. 11 May 2017. http://www.bl.uk/learning/langlit/poetryperformance/rossetti/josephinehart/aboutrossetti.html

Dylan, Bob. "Bob Dylan – Nobel Laureate." *Nobelprize.org.* Nobel Media AB 2014. Web. 14 December 2017. https://www.nobelprize.org/nobel_prizes/literature/laureates/2016/dylan-lecture.html

Gorton, Lisa. "John Donne's Use of Space." *Early Modern Literary Studies* 4.2. Special Issue 3 (1998): 9.1 – 27. OCLC. Web. Date accessed. https://extra.shu.ac.uk/emls/04-2/gortjohn.htm

King, Dr Bill. *Shakespeare in the Alley: Bob Dylan's Poetics.* PRX.org, 2004. Web. 16 October 2017. https://exchange.prx.org/series/26877-shakespeare-in-the-alley-bob-dylan-s-poetics

O'Hagan, Andrew. "The people's poet". *The Guardian.* Sunday 20 January 2008. Web. 20 September 2017. https://www.theguardian.com/books/2008/jan/19/poetry.classics

"Pastoral: Poetic Term." *poets.org.* 16 December 2011. Web. 10 August 2017. https://www.poets.org/poetsorg/text/pastoral-poetic-term

Sproxton, Judy. *Love Poetry from the Early Sonnets to the Seventeenth Century.* London: Duckworth, 2000.

Vendler, Helen. *The Art of Shakespeare's Sonnets.* Cambridge, Mass: Belknap Press of Harvard University Press, 1997.

Wilde, Oscar. "The Critic as Artist." *Oscar Wilde online.* Web. 15 October 2017. http://www.wilde-online.info/the-critic-as-artist-page44.html

Acknowledgements

I am heavily indebted to my editor Luke Allan for working my unkempt manuscript into a discourse which I believe does justice to such beautiful poems.

I thank my dear friends Victor Nicoli, Sue Emmett and Elana O'Loskey for their uplifting and everlasting support and encouragement. And I express my deep gratitude to Integrative GP Dr Nadine Perlen for restoring my health, enabling me to write this book.

Also by Sandra Roe

Poems from the Swan Coastal Plain

These poems reflect the experience of living in Western Australia's Perth, the world's most isolated city. The city lies on an ancient landscape, surrounding the old, quiet, beautiful Swan River.

Also looking outward, Western Australians are keen world travellers, and some of these poems are inspired by travel in Italy.

If you enjoyed
How Love Poems Work…

I would really, really appreciate it if you would help others to enjoy it, too. Reviews help to persuade other readers to read my books. More readers encourages me to write more and that means there will be more for you to enjoy. You can place a review for How Love Poems Work by visiting amazon.com.

ABOUT SANDRA ROE

Sandra Roe lives in Perth, the capital city of Western Australia, where she writes poetry, books about poetry, and edits fiction. She has a BA and MA Preliminary in English Literature from the University of Western Australia and a Graduate Diploma in Information and Library Studies from Curtin University. She has worked as a teacher, a journalist and a cataloguing librarian. She is based online at www.sandra-roe.com. You can connect with Sandra on Facebook (Sandra Roe – Author) if you have something to say or a question to ask.

Printed in Great Britain
by Amazon